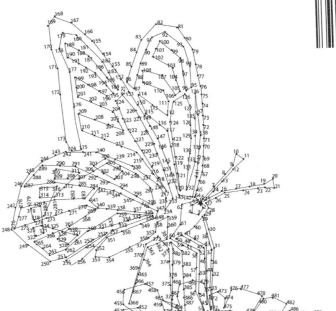

Challenging Dot-to-Dots for Adults
Puzzles from 410 to 593 Dots

By Puzzle Master

WELCOME!

We invite you to relax with the beautiful images

found in these pages whether this is your first

or 100th dot to dot book.

The directions are simple: Start with dot #1,

and draw a line to dot #2, then a line from dot #2

to dot #3, and so on. A picture will appear

as you connect the dots.

Take all the time you need and don't worry,

you will always find the next dot,

even if you don't see it at first.

We hope you enjoy this

super challenging dot to dot book.

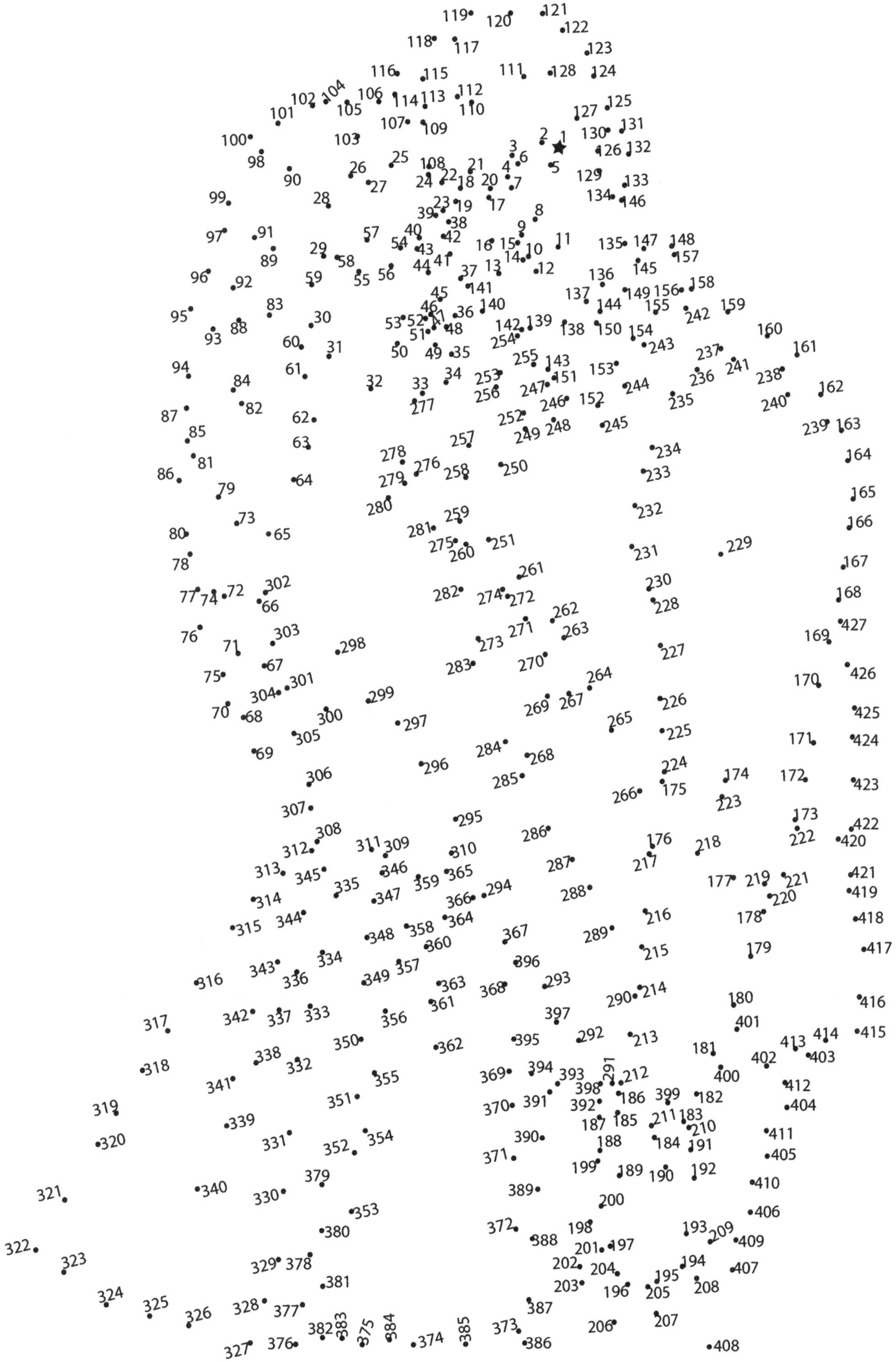

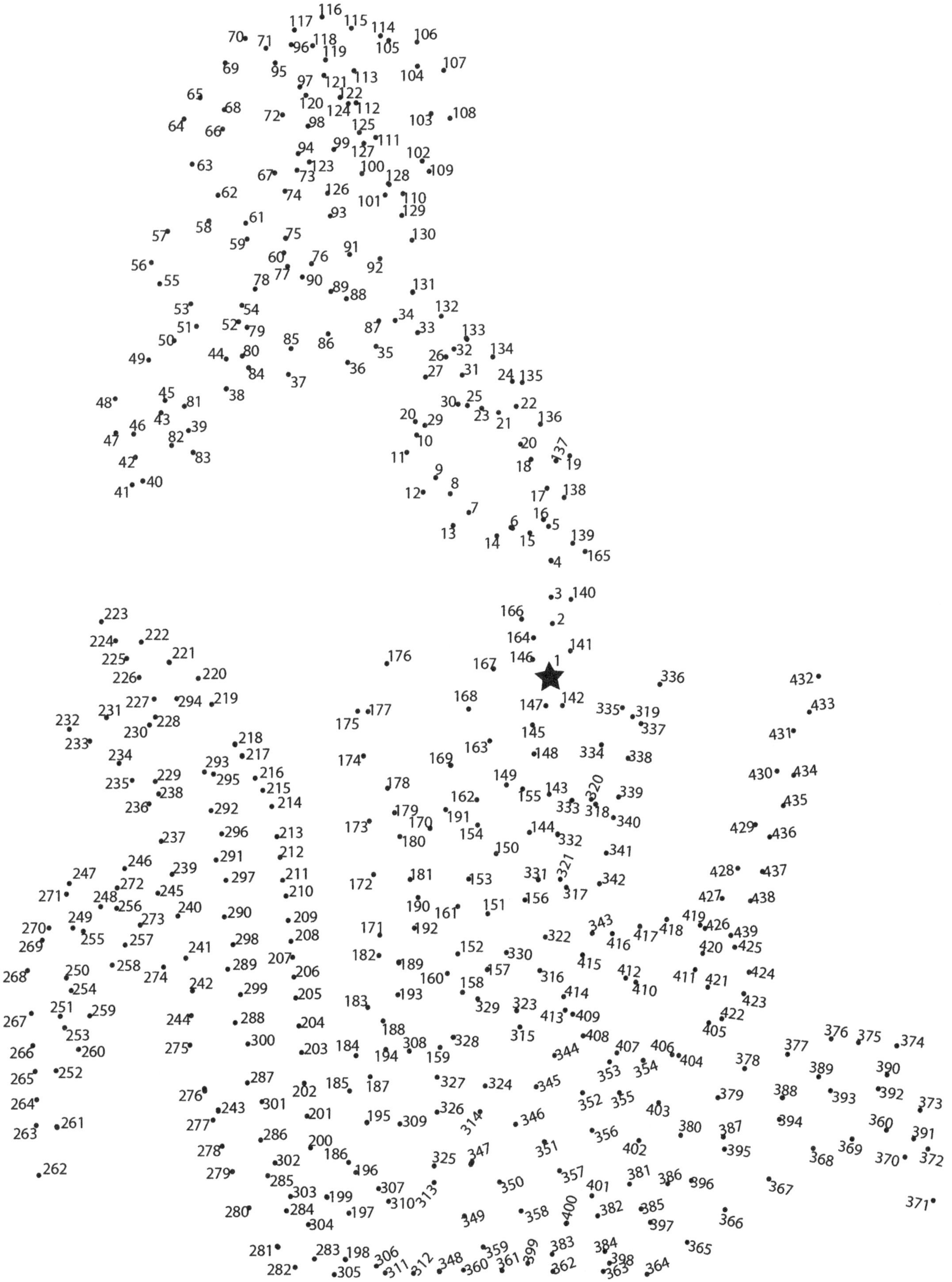

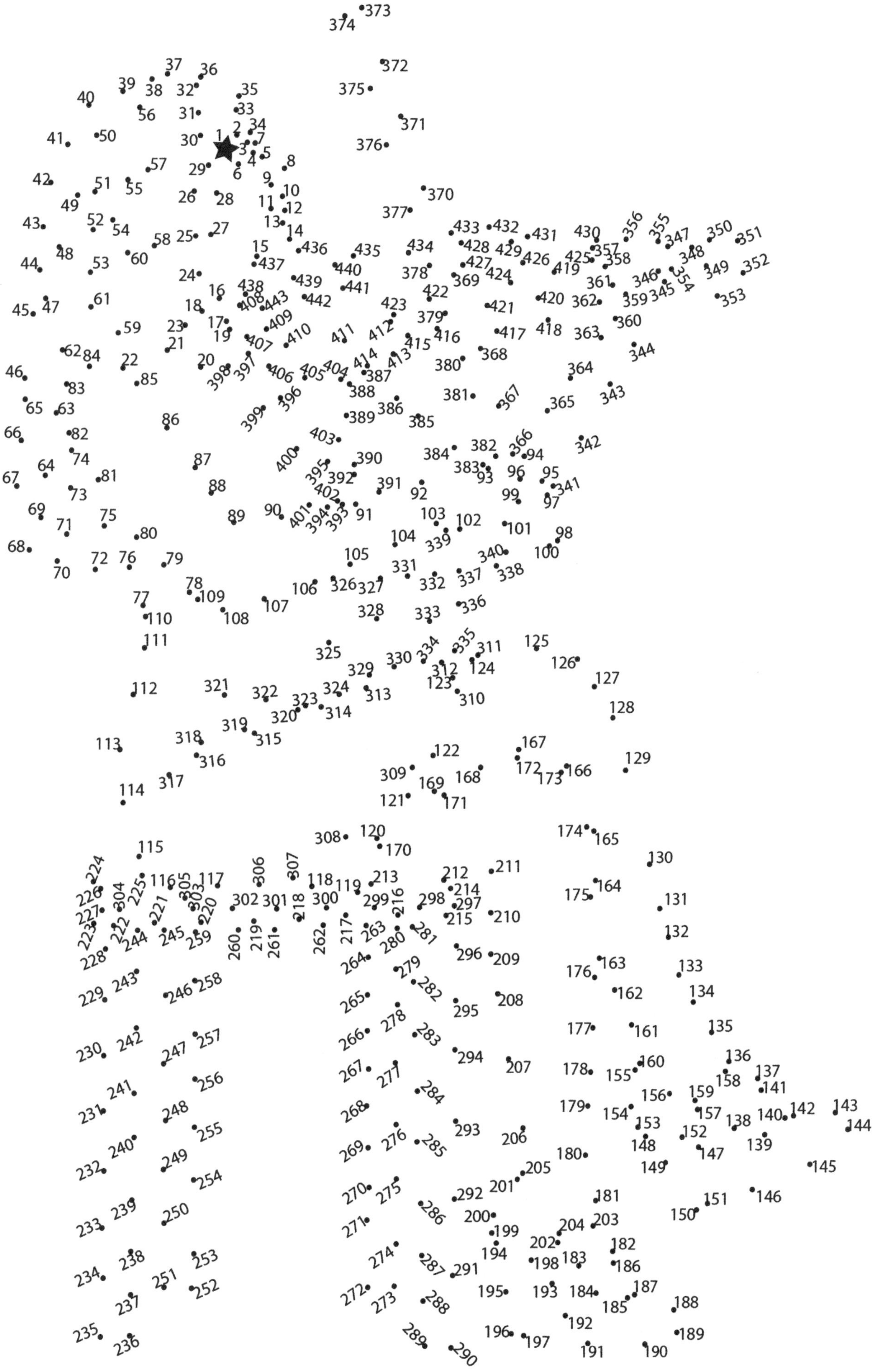

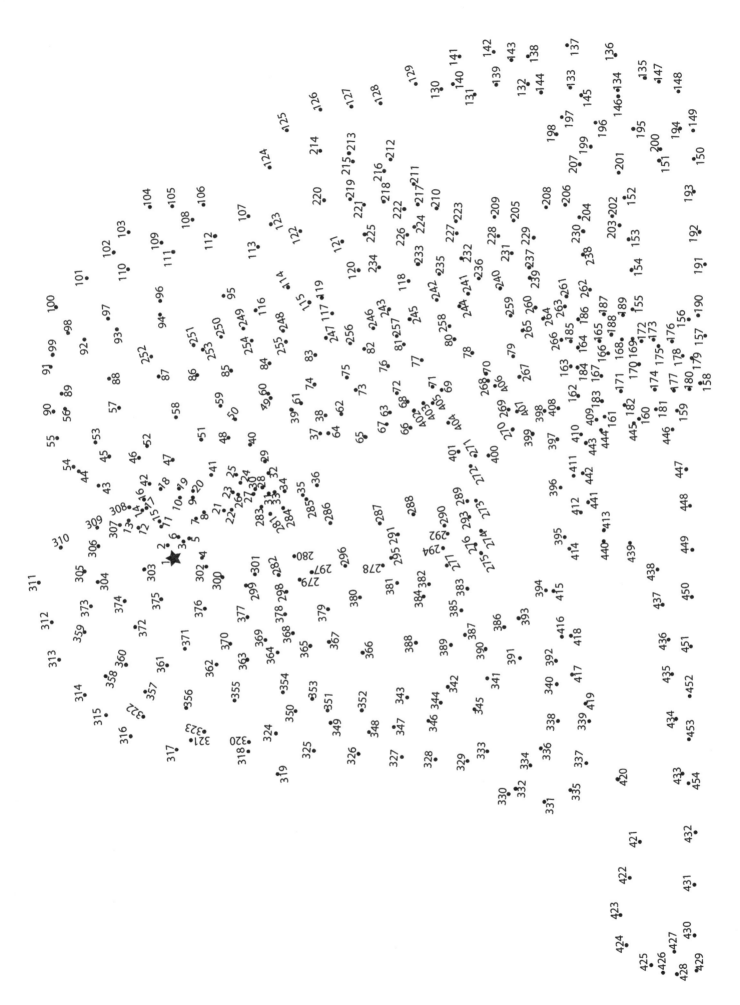

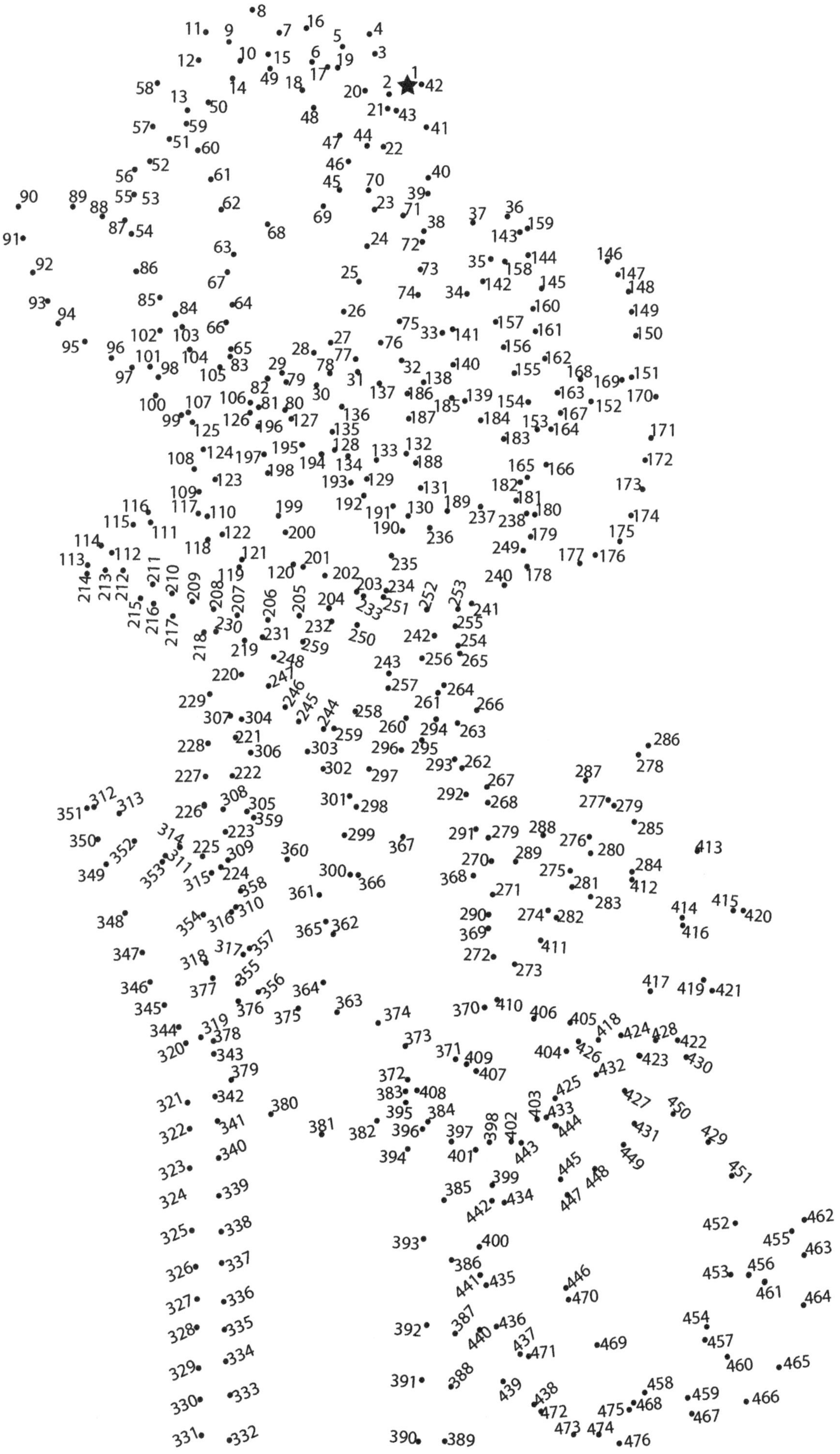

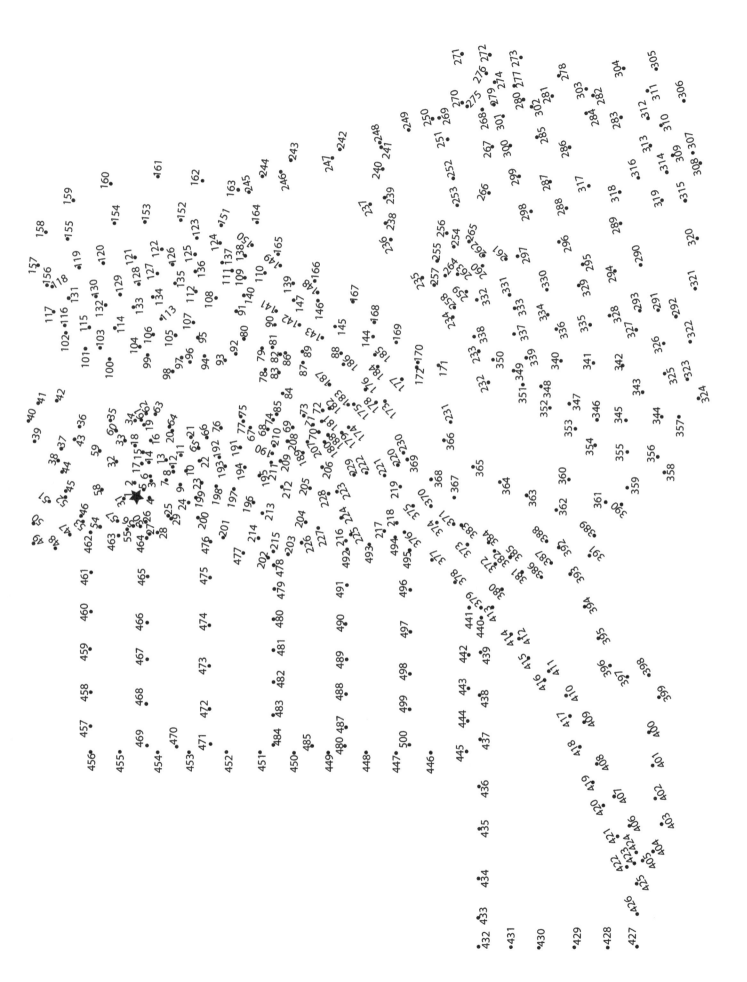

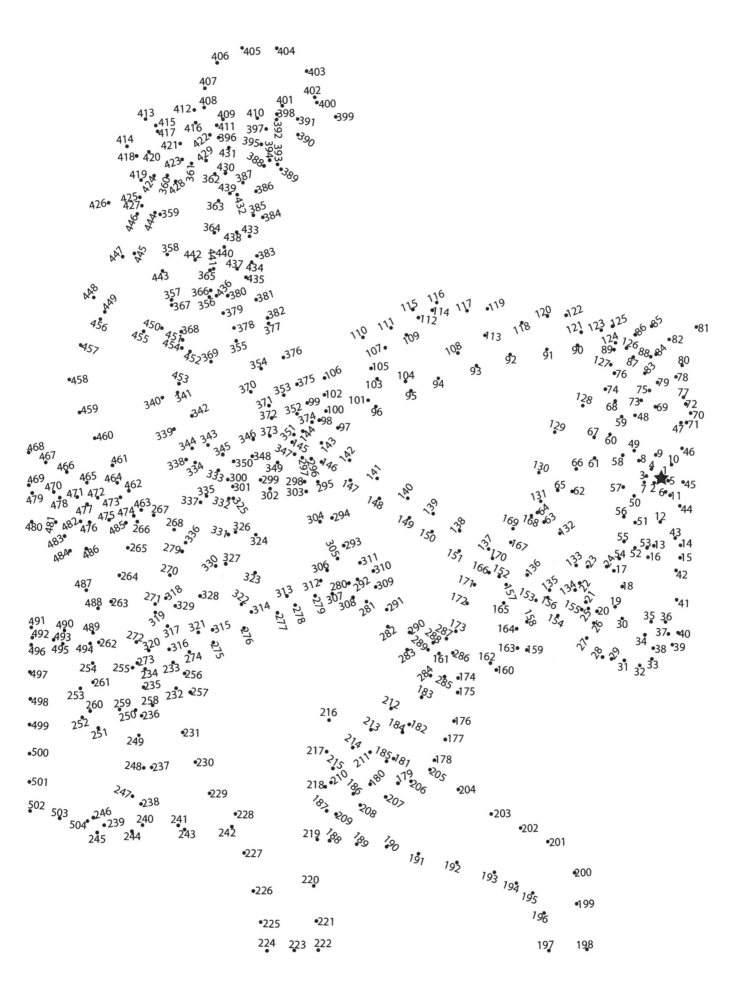

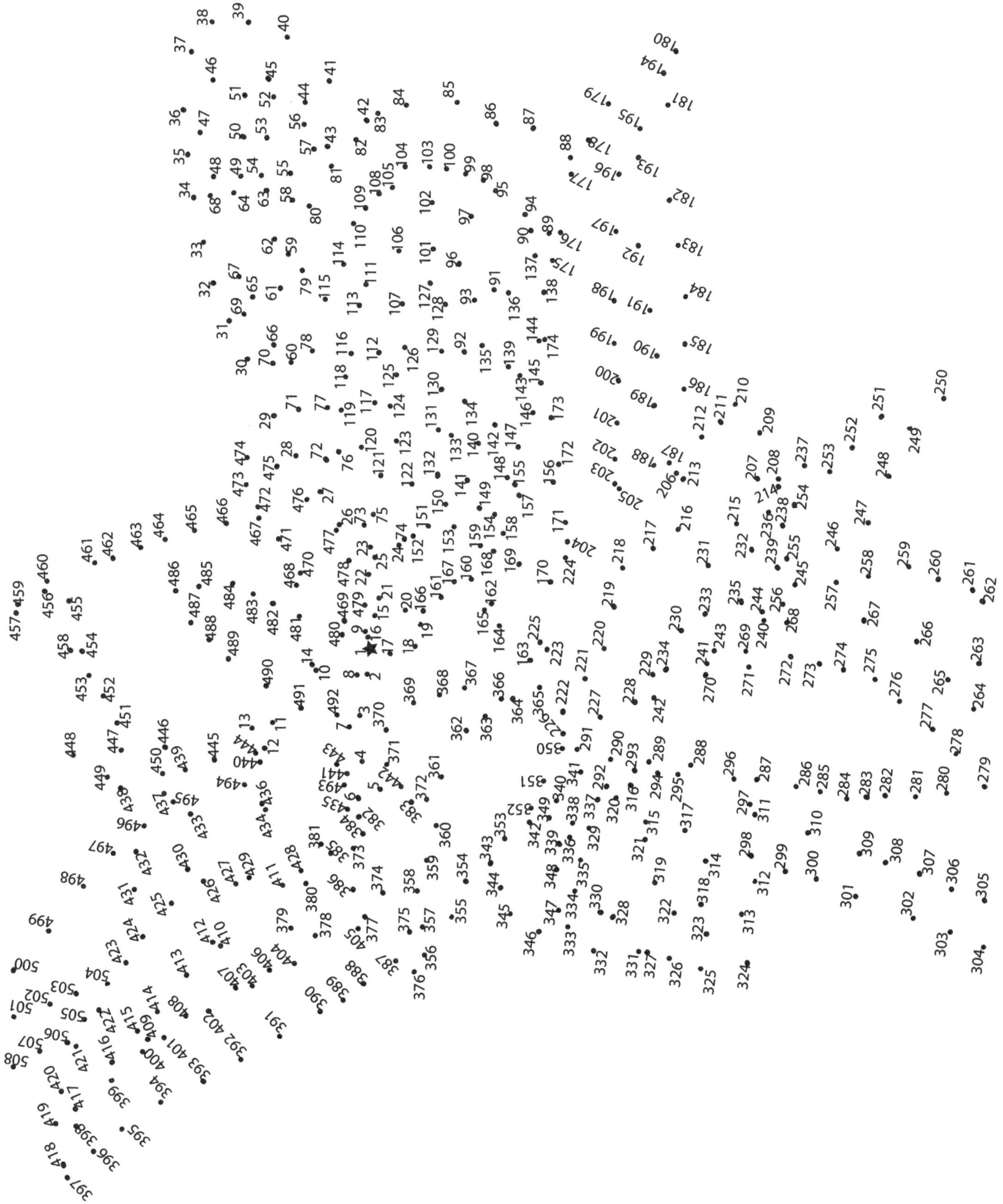

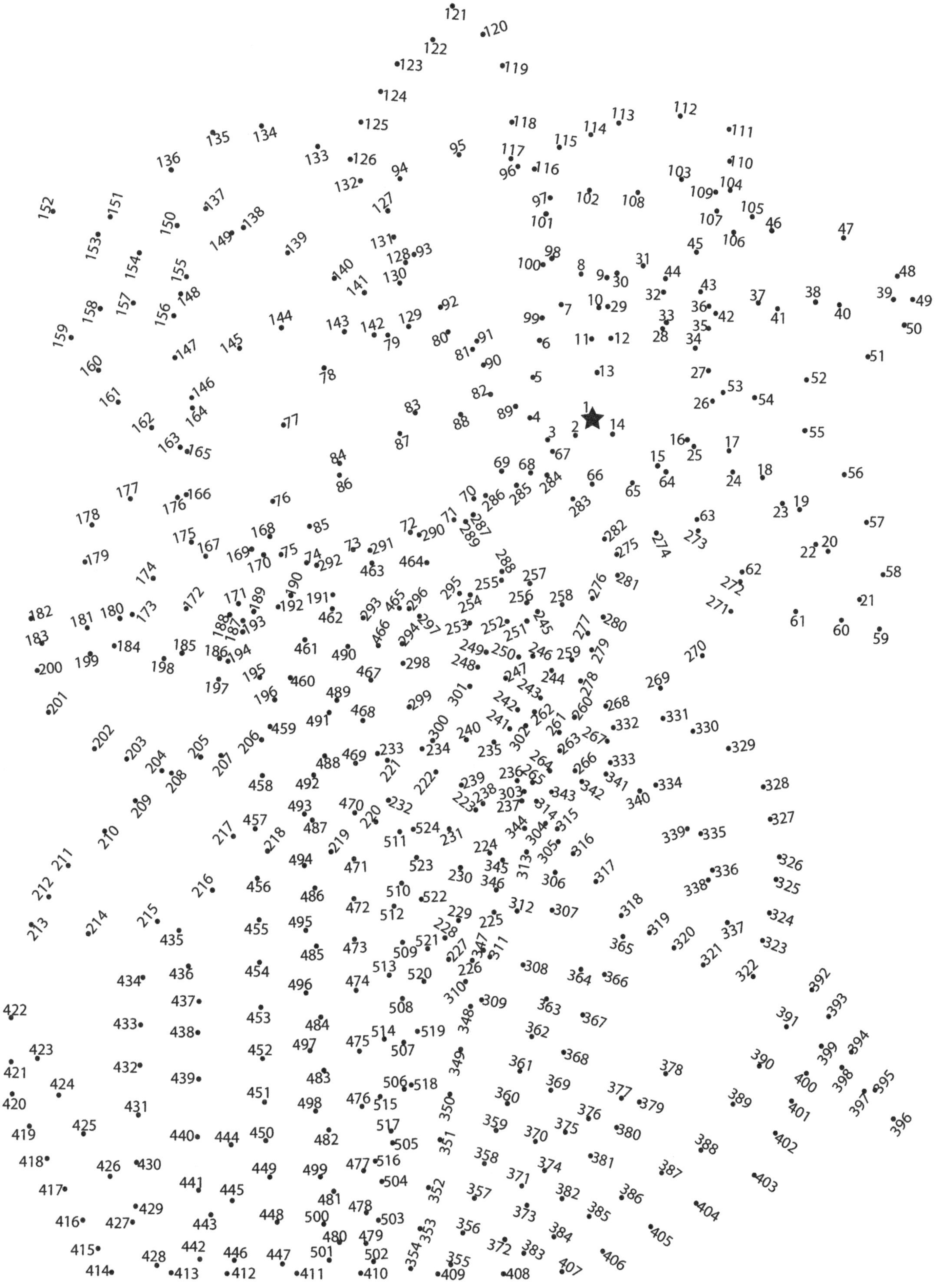

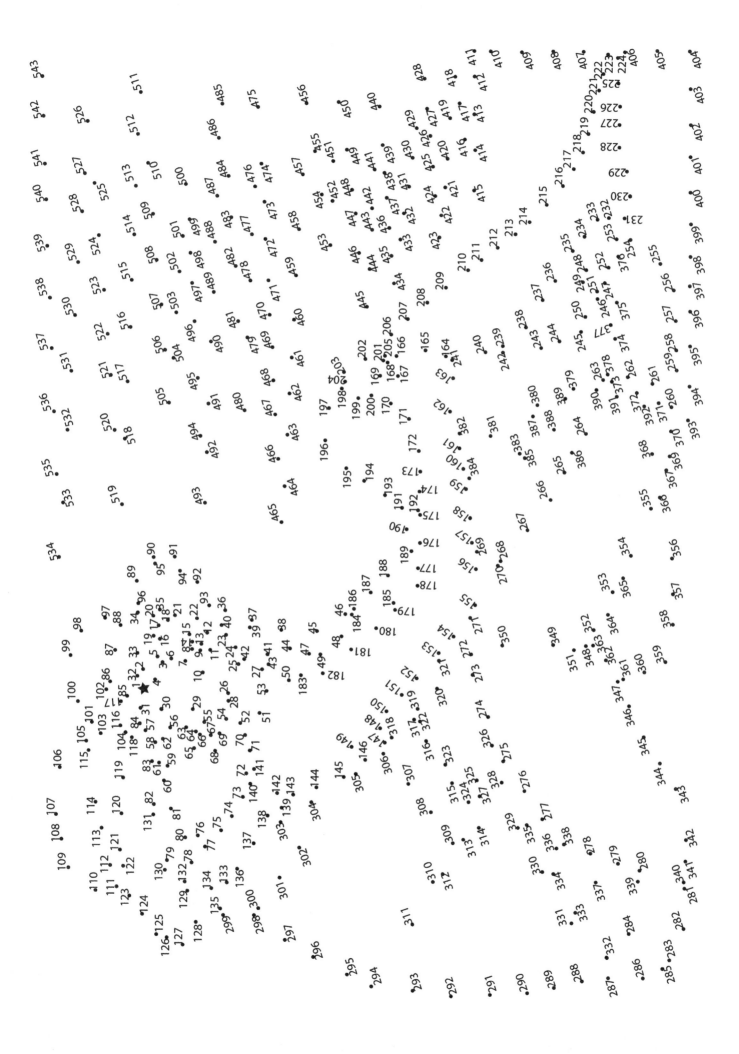

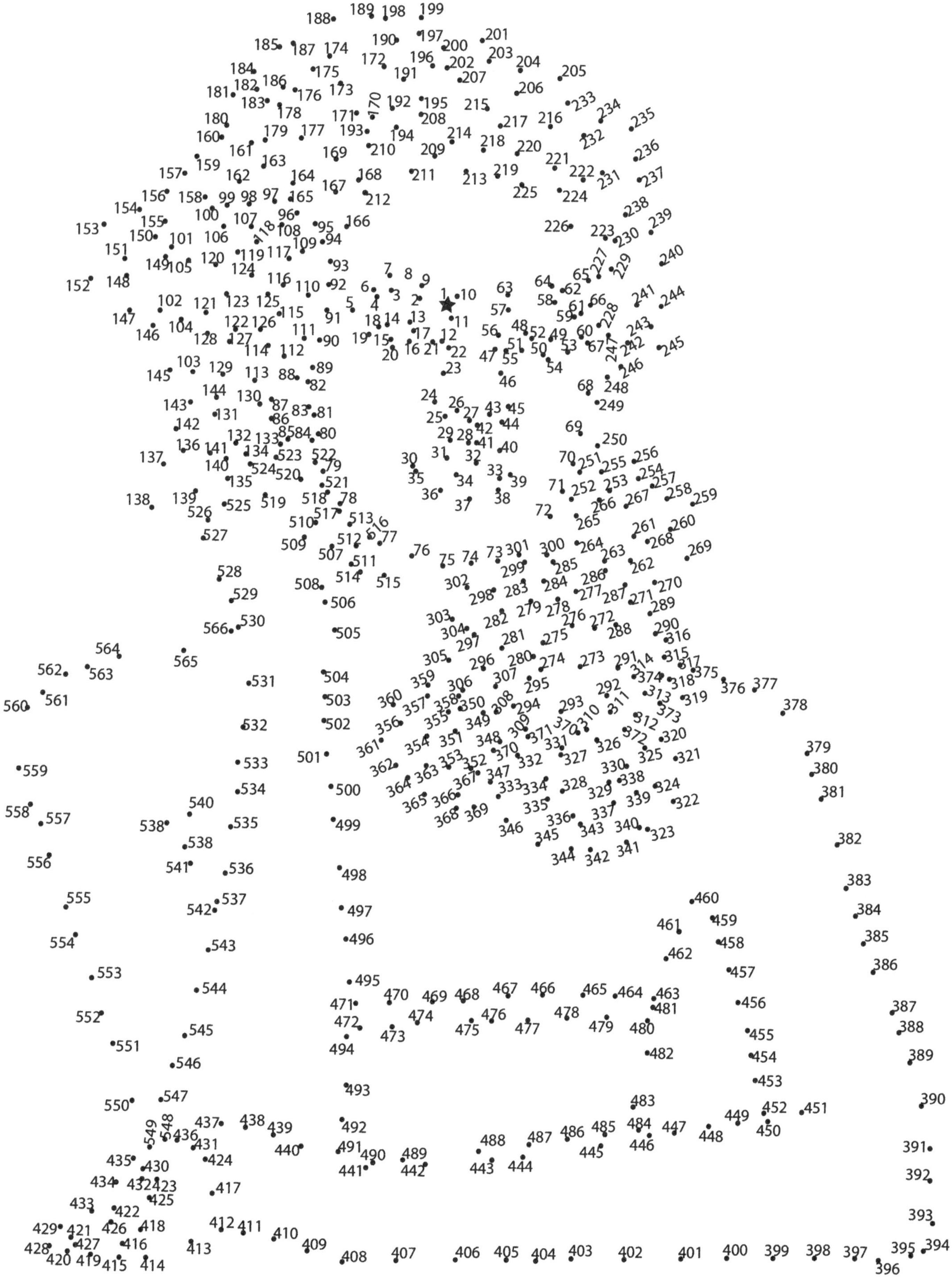

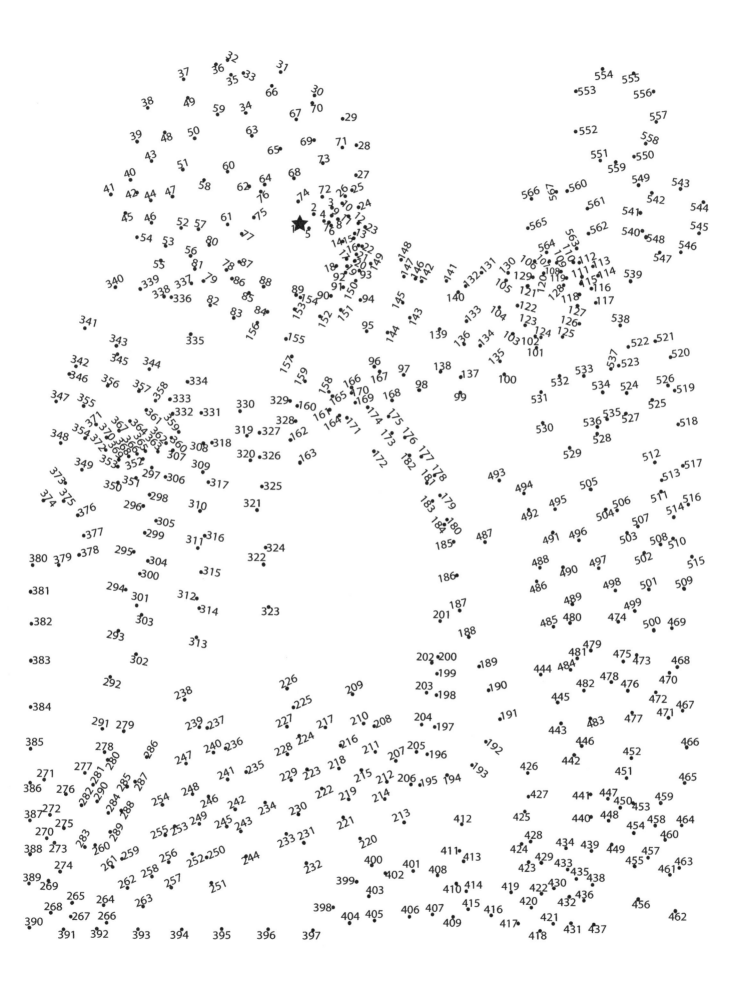

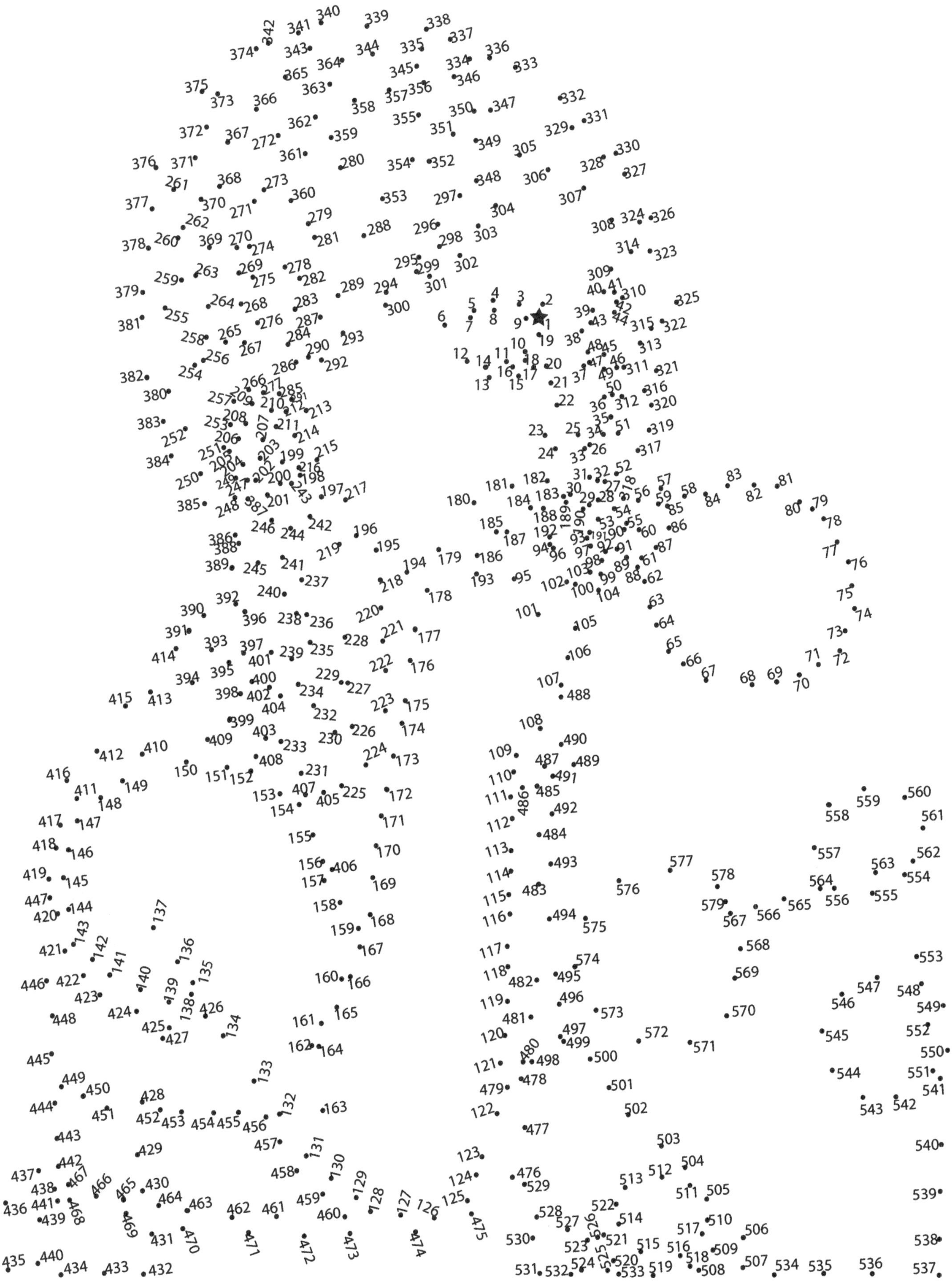

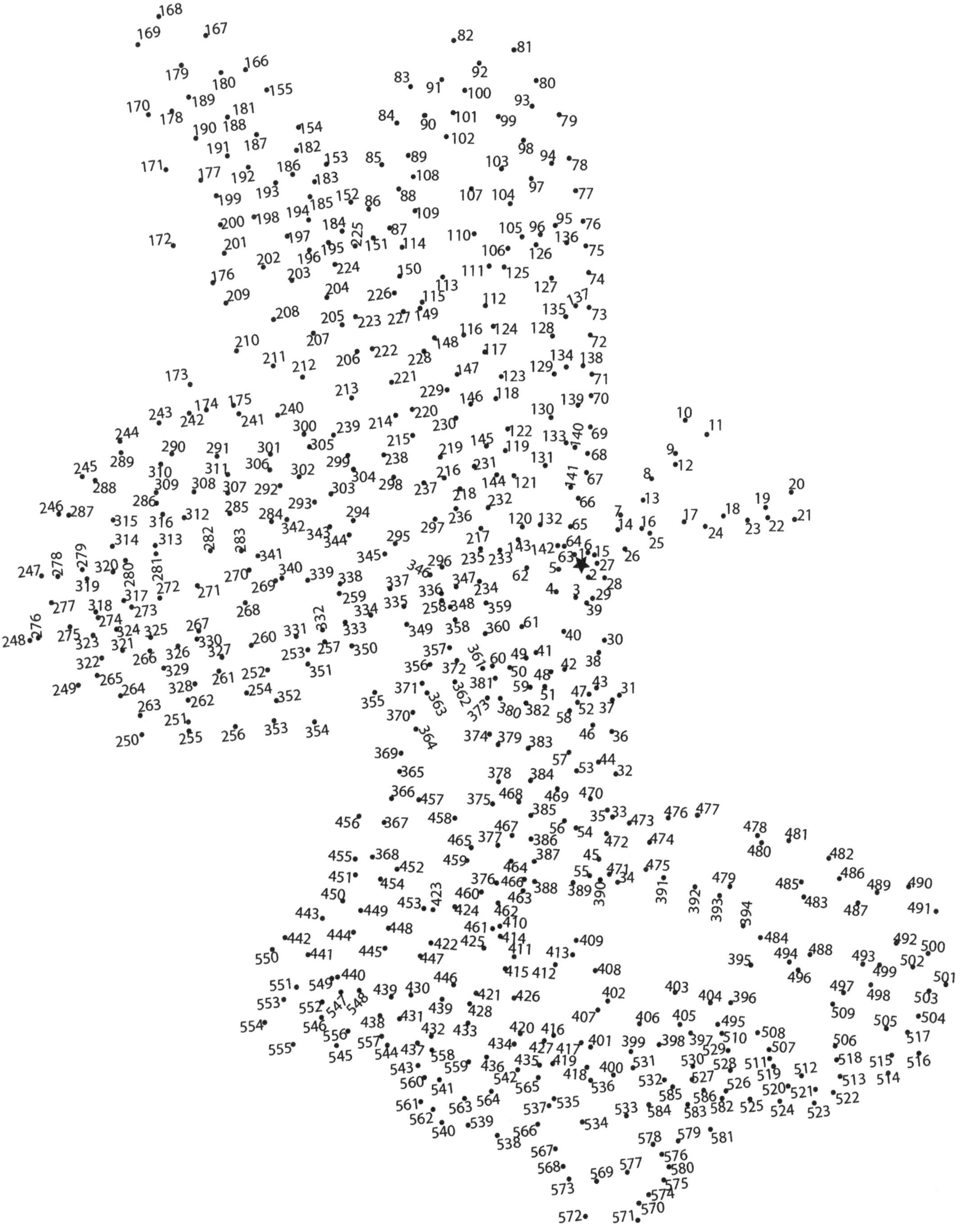

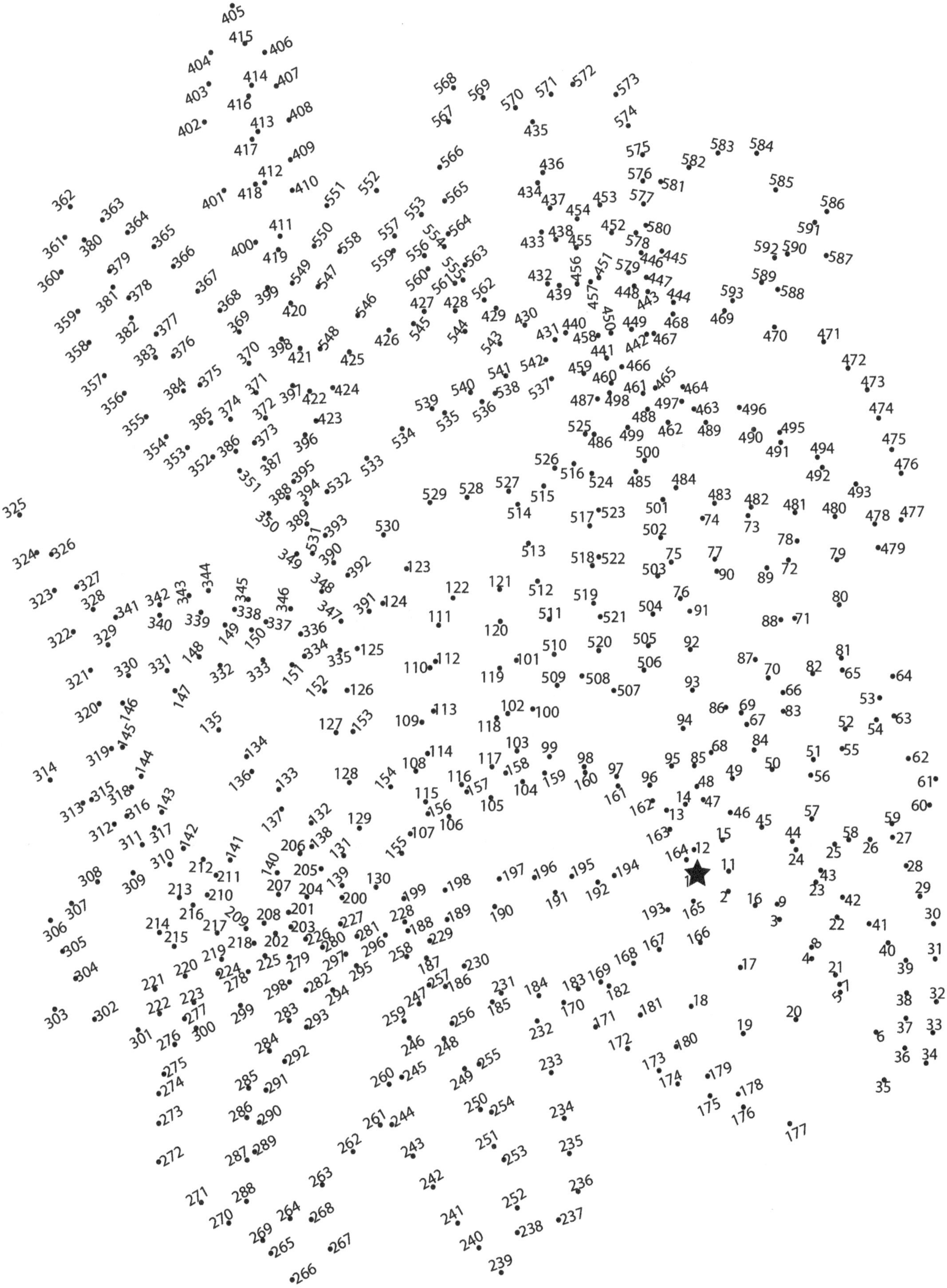

Answer Key

(start from top left to right)

1

2

3

4

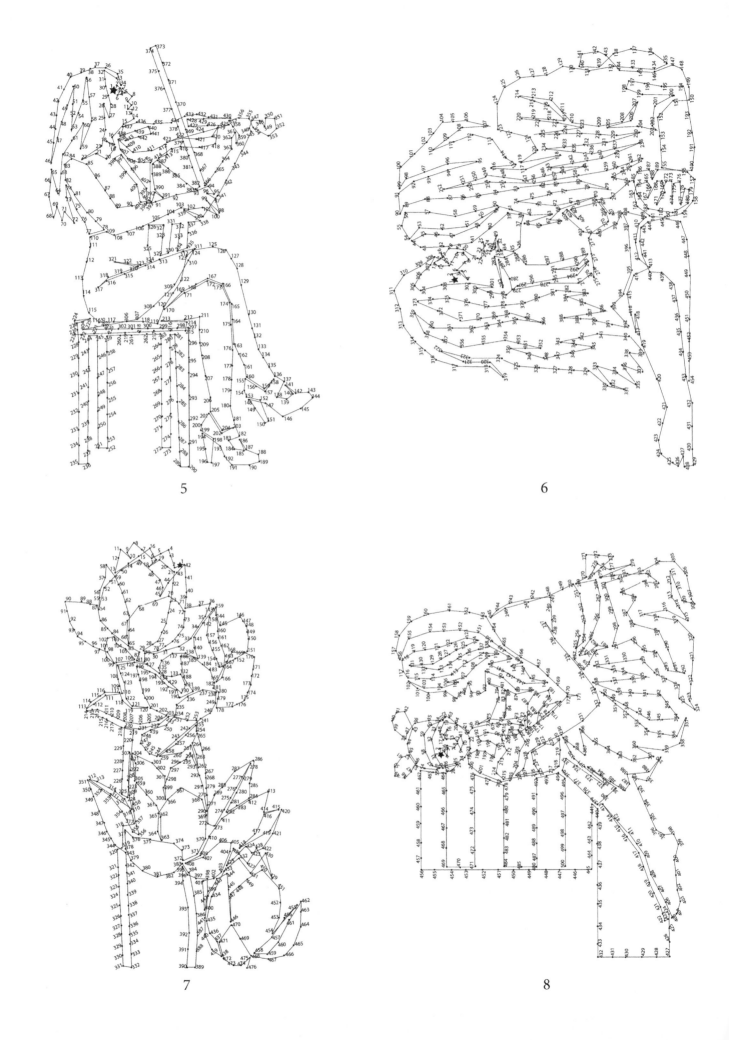

5

6

7

8

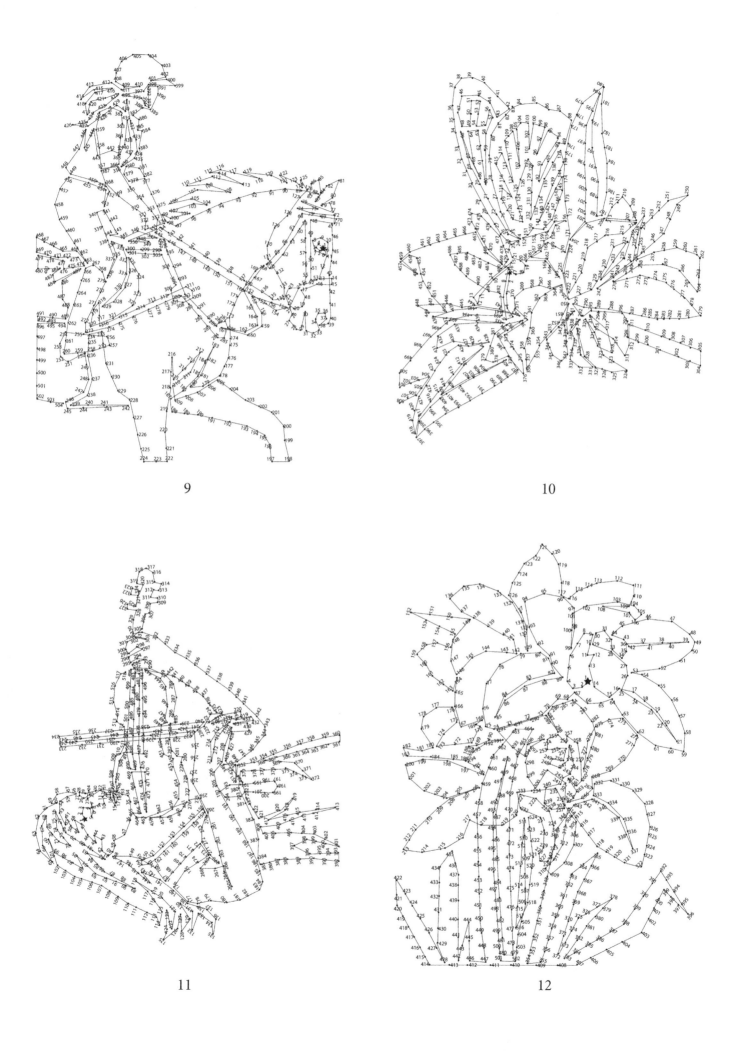

9

10

11

12

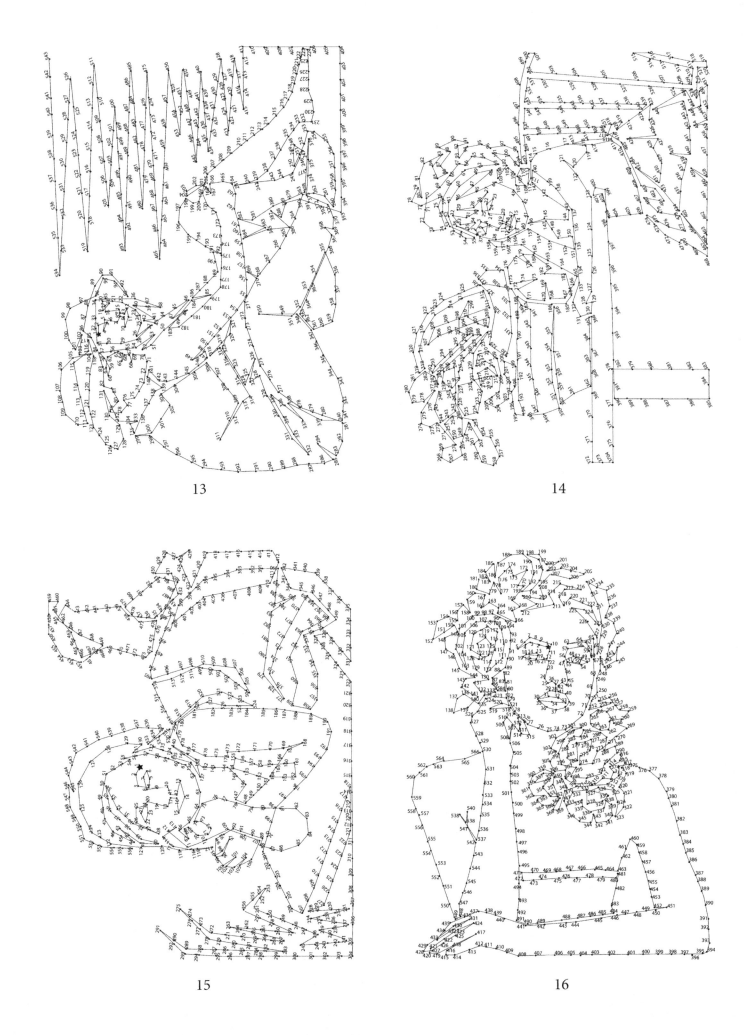

13

14

15

16

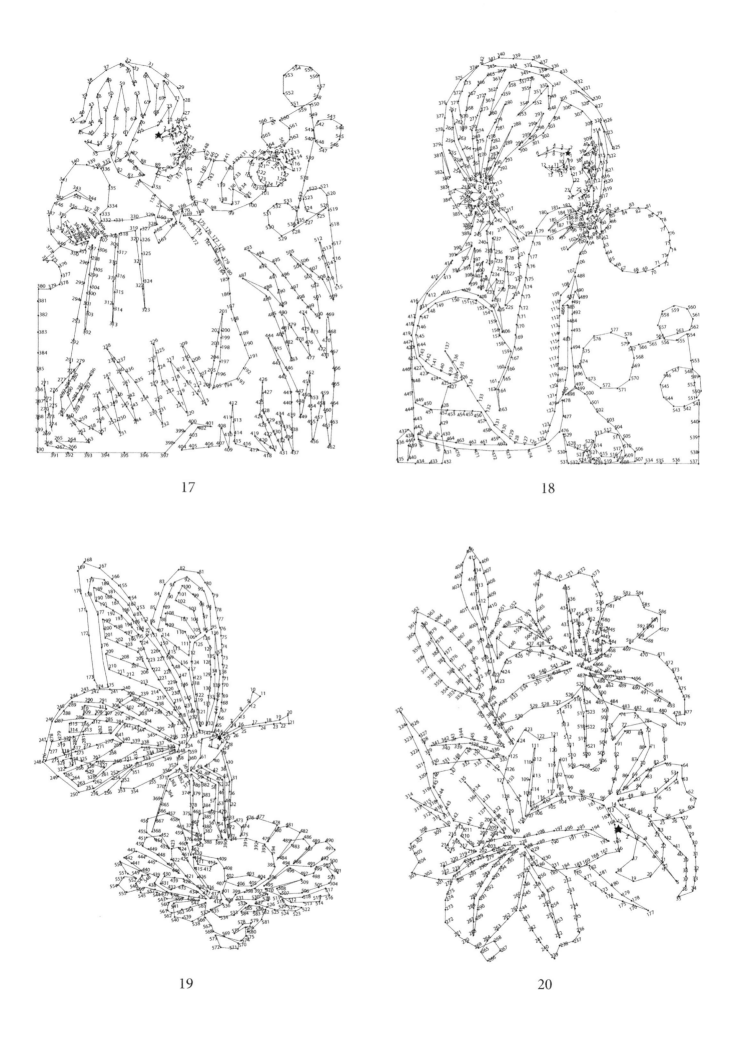

17

18

19

20

Please Leave Us A Review On Amazon!

Made in the USA
Monee, IL
18 November 2024

70399484R00031